A PARRAGON BOOK

Published by Parragon Books, Unit 13-17 Avonbridge Trading Estate,
Atlantic Road, Avonmouth, Bristol BS11 9QD
Produced by The Templar Company plc, Pippbrook Mill,
London Road, Dorking, Surrey RH4 1JE
Copyright © 1994 Parragon Book Service Limited
Designed by Janie Louise Hunt
Edited by Caroline Steeden
Printed and bound in Italy
ISBN 1-85813-946-5

This Book
Belongs to

_____

_____

CONTENTS

BULKY THE GIANT

WRITTEN BY GEOFF COWAN

As giants go, Bulky was okay. He was what you might call a gentle giant. He was always polite to the local villagers. He did his very best not to upset them, which, being huge, wasn't easy.

Take Bulky's feet, for instance. His shoes seemed like boats to the villagers. Even if Bulky tiptoed past their homes, he still made the ground tremble. The startled folk fell out of bed, kitchen crockery rattled and furniture bounced about.

The villagers complained to Bulky. They only dared to because he was so nice and kind. He even said sorry and promised to creep around more carefully than before.

"I should think so," said the villagers, impatiently.

Then there was his sneezing. Now everyone sneezes from time to time, and giants are no different. But when Bulky sneezed he sent such a blast of air howling across the valley, the villagers had to rush indoors for fear of being blown away!

They complained to Bulky about that as
well. The giant promised he would sneeze
into his hanky, which, after all, is only the polite
thing to do. But sometimes a sneeze came upon him
all of a sudden, before he could do anything about it.

11

One complaint followed another. Eventually the villagers decided life would be much more comfortable without a giant living on their doorstep. So they sent for Spellbound the Wizard and asked him if he could shrink Bulky down to normal human size. Bulky agreed to the plan at once, proving what a big-hearted giant he was!

"Abracadabra, pots, pans and sink,

A wave of my wand will make Bulky shrink!"

As Spellbound chanted the rhyme he gave his wand a few extra waves for luck. Sometimes, his spells needed it!

All at once, a silvery mist appeared, hiding Bulky from sight. When it cleared, the delighted villagers saw that Bulky was just the same size as them!

For a while everyone lived peacefully. Bulky moved in with a kind family who looked after him very well, and he began to enjoy life at his new size.

Now life's full of little surprises but the surprise that arrived from beyond the mountains surrounding the villagers' valley was big as in giant; the walking, talking type, just like Bulky used to be!

Heavyhand was short-tempered and always wanted to get his own way. The villagers didn't know this at first. But they soon found out. When Heavyhand lay down for a snooze in a lush, green meadow, sending sheep scattering, the villagers complained, just as they had to Bulky.

But Heavyhand roared angrily at them and warned that if he wasn't left in peace, he would flatten every home in the village! Then he banged his fist mightily on the ground. The frightened villagers jumped into the air, and scattered in all directions.

"Clear off!" he bellowed. "I like this valley and I'm here to stay!"

From that day on, Heavyhand stomped about wherever he pleased, flattening crops, and knocking down trees. When he lay down for a rest, he always slipped off his boots and used them as a pillow. He had horribly smelly feet, and the rotten pong wafted through the valley, sending everyone indoors, rushing to shut their doors and windows. And when he slept, he snored louder than thunder. The villagers huddled in their homes, holding their heads and wishing Heavyhand would go away. But he wouldn't.

It wasn't long before they began to wish something else.

"If only Bulky were still big, he'd soon see off Heavyhand!" sighed one.

"It's our own silly fault," agreed a second.

"We shouldn't have been so selfish," said a third. "Bulky was such a thoughtful, kind and good-tempered giant. He never did anyone any harm!"

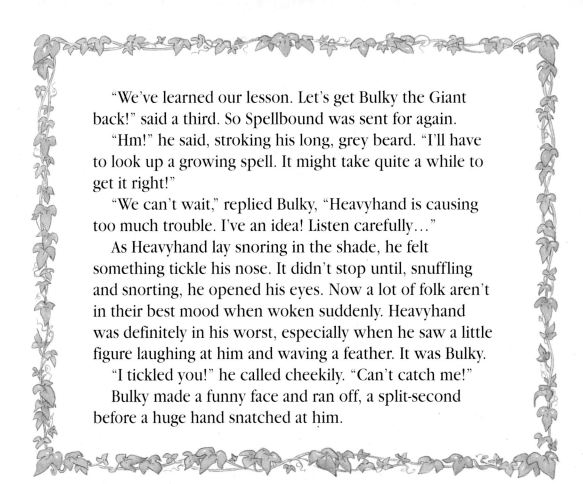

"We've learned our lesson. Let's get Bulky the Giant back!" said a third. So Spellbound was sent for again.

"Hm!" he said, stroking his long, grey beard. "I'll have to look up a growing spell. It might take quite a while to get it right!"

"We can't wait," replied Bulky, "Heavyhand is causing too much trouble. I've an idea! Listen carefully…"

As Heavyhand lay snoring in the shade, he felt something tickle his nose. It didn't stop until, snuffling and snorting, he opened his eyes. Now a lot of folk aren't in their best mood when woken suddenly. Heavyhand was definitely in his worst, especially when he saw a little figure laughing at him and waving a feather. It was Bulky.

"I tickled you!" he called cheekily. "Can't catch me!"

Bulky made a funny face and ran off, a split-second before a huge hand snatched at him.

Bulky jumped onto a horse he'd left nearby, and galloped towards the mountains, while a furious Heavyhand reached for his boots. But some of the villagers had tied the laces together and by the time Heavyhand had unknotted them, Bulky had reached the mouth of an enormous cave.

He didn't try to hide, but waited till Heavyhand had seen him before disappearing inside, with Heavyhand in hot pursuit! Bulky had found the cave long ago, during his days as a giant. He knew another way out, if you were small enough. Now, of course, he was! Bulky scrambled out into the fresh air.

The villagers were ready for their part of the plan!

As Bulky rode clear, they pushed against a rock high above the cave mouth, heaving and shoving until they set it rolling down the mountain, loosening others as it went, until an avalanche fell across the front of the cave. Heavyhand had no time to escape.

"He's trapped inside!" cried the villagers.

But not for long!

How the mountain trembled as Heavyhand raged and cursed, as he began to dig himself out. He worked all day and night. So did Spellbound, until at last his spell was ready. The wizard's wand whirled and he muttered strange magic words. A dazzling arc of stars appeared around Bulky who began to grow and grow, just as Heavyhand came bursting from the cave.

Imagine his surprise when he saw Bulky standing a good head and broad shoulders above him. Even for a giant, Bulky was big.

"Go and find your own valley. This one's mine!" roared Bulky, raising his voice for the first time in his life.

None of the villagers minded one bit. They were only too pleased to see good old Bulky back to normal. Heavyhand took off nervously across the mountains without looking back.

"We promise never to complain again, Bulky," the thankful villagers told him. "We know we made a big mistake before!"

"More like a giant one!" someone joked and everyone laughed, though Bulky took care not to laugh too loudly!

21

THE LOST GIANT

WRITTEN BY AMBER HUNT

The air wobbled a bit, shimmered, swirled and with a 'whoomph' a rather bewildered, twelve-foot giant appeared. He was only a very young giant, and looked rather like any other young boy — except he was slightly larger, of course!

"Oh dear," said the giant, stepping on a bush and flattening it. Turning round he bumped into a tree, which bent over at an alarming angle.

"Hello," said a tiny voice.

"What was that?!" said the giant, startled. He whirled round looking for the voice and knocked the tree right over. "Where am I?"

"Stand still," yelled the small voice. "You're in our farmyard. I suspect you are all my fault!"

"Pardon?" said the giant. "Did you say I'm all your fault?"

"Yes," yelled the small voice, "Only could you whisper because you are deafening me."

"Of course," apologised the giant and stepping back he trod in the pond and got his socks wet.

"Stand still please, before you demolish the whole farmyard," pleaded the voice.

"Where are you?" asked the giant.

"I'm down here, by the well. Perhaps if you bend down, carefully, you might be able to see me."

And so, carefully, the giant bent down and peered at the well. Standing next to it was a little boy with blond hair and very dirty knees.

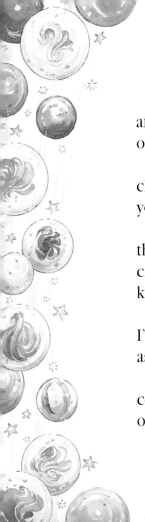

"Oh," said the giant. "You're a little boy … aren't you afraid of me? All the little boys in my story books are afraid of giants." "No, I'm not afraid," said the little boy.

The giant got down on his hands and knees to get a closer look. "Gosh, your knees are dirty," he said. "Have you been playing?"

The little boy looked at his knees. "Um, yes, I suppose they are a bit dirty. I lost my magic marble and was crawling around looking for it. This is a farmyard you know, so it gets a bit muddy."

"Oh," breathed the giant. "Have you got a magic marble? I've got one too. Here look," and he fished a marble as big as a doughnut out of his pocket.

"Wow," said the little boy. "That's wonderful. I wish I could find mine." Then a thought crossed his mind. "How old are you?" he asked the giant.

"Seventy," replied the giant.

"Oh," said the little boy, clearly disappointed.

"But I think ten giant years are the same as one of your years, so I suppose I'm about seven in your world."

"I'm seven too!" said the little boy. "That's terrific! You know what, I think my marble magicked you here. I was wishing for someone to play with when the air went wobbly. I was so scared I dropped my marble, which was why I was crawling around in the mud looking for it — and then you appeared. What's your name?" he asked. "Mine's Oliver."

"I'm Bertie," said the giant. "I was wishing for a friend on my marble too," and they looked at each other in awe.

"Wow," they breathed together. "Weird!"

Just then a voice called from inside the farmhouse, "Oliver, Oliver!"

"Oh no," said Oliver, "that's my mum. You'd better hide quickly." Oliver looked at his large friend. Where on earth do you hide a twelve-foot giant?

"I've got it," he said, "in the barn. Follow me — very carefully."

Oliver ran across the yard, with Bertie following — carefully. They went down past the stables, across the cornfield and into the meadow where the hay barn was.

"Oliver, Oliver, where are you? It's lunchtime." His mum's voice floated across the meadow.

"Quick, help me with this door," panted Oliver. Bertie heaved open the hay barn door and dived inside.

"Good, there's plenty of space. Hide over there in that corner. Well, as best you can, anyway. I have to go and have my lunch," Oliver explained to Bertie, "then I'll come back. Are you hungry?" he added.

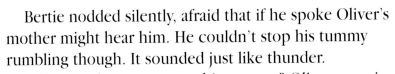

Bertie nodded silently, afraid that if he spoke Oliver's mother might hear him. He couldn't stop his tummy rumbling though. It sounded just like thunder.

"I'll try and get you something to eat," Oliver promised and off he went, back to the house for lunch. He gobbled his lunch up as quickly as he could. He could hardly wait to get back to the barn and see his new friend. As soon as he had finished eating he rushed back to Bertie.

He had brought Bertie a jam sandwich, which he'd hidden in his pocket. Bertie ate it in one bite. He was too polite to tell Oliver that giants make their sandwiches as big as double beds.

"Now," said Oliver, "we have to find my marble and a way to get you back home. You're too big to stay here and Dad said he had some work to do later in the barn — so we'd better hurry."

Bertie and Oliver crept out of the barn and back to the well. They both got down on their hands and knees and started searching for the marble. They searched and searched, but found nothing.

Eventually Bertie said, "I'm thirsty. Is there any water in your well?" He peered over the edge.

"No," said Oliver, "it's been filled in."

"Wait a minute," yelled the giant, causing the ground to shake and the trees to sway dangerously, "I think I've found it! There's something shining in the earth, about three feet down." He reached his long arm into the well, fished around a bit and brought out — the marble!

"Hooray! You've found it!" cried Oliver.

"Wow," gasped Bertie. "It's beautiful."

"Right, back to the barn," said Oliver excitedly. "It's time for some magic!"

Back in the barn Oliver and Bertie sat and rubbed their
marbles and tried all the magic words they could think of,
but the air didn't move, no 'whoomph' sound happened
and Bertie stayed firmly in the barn with Oliver.

"Bertie," said Oliver, "would you like to swap marbles —
like best friends do? We might even find a way to visit each
other." Bertie nodded, smiling enthusiastically. "I'd like
you to visit me in the land of the giants," he said.

In the distance Oliver could hear a tractor. "Oh no,"
he said. "I think my dad might be coming. We have
to think of something, quickly!"

They rubbed the marbles harder and started to
invent magic words and all the time the
tractor was getting nearer. How would
Oliver explain keeping a
twelve-foot giant in the barn?

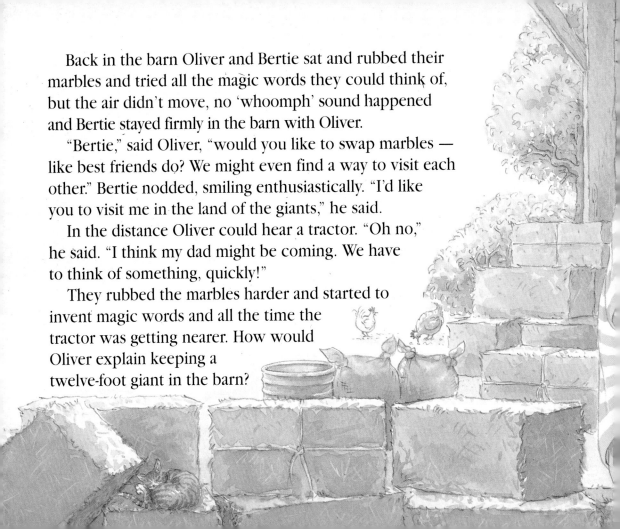

Then Bertie had an idea. "The air went 'whoomph' when I arrived, didn't it? So perhaps if we made the noise backwards it might magic me home."

Oliver and Bertie looked at each other.

"Bye," said Oliver, rubbing his eyes. "See you again?"

"Bye," said Bertie, sniffing. "I'll come back soon."

Oliver and Bertie rubbed their marbles hard, and together they said "Phmoohw." The air wobbled and shimmered a bit and in a flash Bertie was gone.

Outside the tractor noise stopped and a few seconds later Oliver's dad walked into the barn. "Hello," he said. "What are you doing here? That's a pretty amazing marble," he added, nodding at Oliver's hand.

"Yes it is, isn't it?" Oliver held up the marble, which was as big as a doughnut, for his dad to see. "It's a giant-size one," he said, and smiled secretly to himself.

BIGGER, BIGGEST, BEST

WRITTEN BY DAN ABNETT

Fortyodd was a giant. He was called Fortyodd because he was forty-odd times as tall as a man. His hands were as big as bulldozers and his feet were as big as barges. He was huge. If you spread your arms out wide, it wouldn't be as wide as his smile.

Fortyodd was a gardener. He looked after the Great Forest. He strode through his forest in the way a farmer marches through his cabbage patch, bending over to prune an oak tree here, leaning down to replant a birch tree there.

Fortyodd liked his job. Fortyodd liked the Great Forest.
He called it his lawn.

One morning, his friend Fiftytimes came round and
knocked on the door of his shed. Fortyodd's shed was
nine times as large as an aircraft hangar, so the echo of
Fiftytimes' knock rolled around the hills
and dales for a week or two.

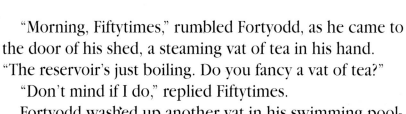

"Morning, Fiftytimes," rumbled Fortyodd, as he came to the door of his shed, a steaming vat of tea in his hand. "The reservoir's just boiling. Do you fancy a vat of tea?"

"Don't mind if I do," replied Fiftytimes.

Fortyodd washed up another vat in his swimming pool-sized sink. He used a small evergreen tree as a brush. "Sugar?" he asked.

"Two barrows, please," replied Fiftytimes, making himself comfortable on the sofa. It wasn't a sofa, actually. It was a small hill that Fortyodd had dragged into the shed and covered with a circus tent, but they called it a sofa.

Fortyodd scooped two wheelbarrows of sugar into Fiftytimes' vat of tea and stirred it with a lamppost.

"So what can I do for you?" Fortyodd asked as they settled down to their vats of tea.

"I thought I had better tell you," said Fiftytimes, "old

Twoscore is planning to enter his prize cabbage in the Harvest Show next week. He's hoping to win the Big Veg prize."

"I didn't know Twoscore had a prize cabbage," said Fortyodd, rather uneasily.

"That's why I thought I'd better tell you," said Fiftytimes. "I was passing his garden just yesterday, and I saw his cabbage patch. It's a handsome crop he's got."

Fortyodd frowned. His brow crinkled so deeply, you could have lost whole flocks of sheep in the wrinkles. You see, every year, his famous pumpkins won the Big Veg rosette at the Harvest Show. There wasn't a giant in the land who grew vegetables that were bigger or better or more beautiful than Fortyodd's pumpkins.

"How are your pumpkins doing this year, anyway?" asked Fiftytimes.

Fortyodd took his friend out into the garden and showed him. There were a dozen splendid pumpkins, each one the size of a hot air balloon.

"Very impressive," said Fiftytimes, "but I have to say, old Twoscore's prize cabbage is bigger than your biggest pumpkin."

Fortyodd was very unhappy. After his friend had gone, he stomped about his garden, grumbling and moaning to himself. The ground shook, and from a mile away it sounded like a serious thunderstorm. Fortyodd tried to do some weeding to take his mind off it, pulling up some chestnut trees, roots and all. But his heart wasn't in it. He went back to his shed and slammed the door behind him.

Fortyodd knew that he had to do something quickly, or Twoscore would win the prize. Fortyodd was very proud of the row of Big Veg rosettes over his fireplace, and couldn't bear the thought that there wouldn't be a new one to pin

up this year. Besides, Big Veg was all he knew. It was his speciality. He hadn't got a particular talent for any of the other prize categories like jam making or tree arranging. Big Veg was his thing. He was a Big Veg giant.

Fortyodd took down the gardening book that his grandfather, old Seventysomething, had compiled. It was chock full of splendid tricks and tips. If nothing else, old Seventysomething had been the tallest gardener of his generation.

Fortyodd laid the book open on his desk. The open book was as wide as the wingspan of a jumbo jet.

Fortyodd put on his reading glasses (two telescope lenses from an observatory held in carefully bent scaffolding) and studied the book carefully, slowly turning the rugby pitch-sized pages.

Finally, just as it was getting dark, he found something.

There on page four thousand and one was a recipe for Plant Growth Formula. It seemed his grandfather had got the recipe from a retired witch.

That evening, Fortyodd made up the recipe. It took hours of careful mixing, measuring and stirring. At last, he was sure he had it pretty much right. He poured the formula out of the cement mixer and into a huge pair of furnace bellows. Then, with his lamp in one hand and the bellows in the other, he went out into the dark, to his pumpkin patch nearby. The pumpkins looked huge and golden in the moonlight.

Fortyodd took the bellows and pumped a spray of formula over his prize vegetables. The magic formula twinkled electric green in the darkness. Satisfied with a job well done, Fortyodd admired his handiwork. Already, the pumpkins looked even more huge and golden. Then Fortyodd went off to bed.

Next morning, Fortyodd's alarm (a church clocktower on the bedside table) woke him at eight, and he was surprised to see that it was still dark. He went to the door and tried to open it, but it wouldn't budge. He went to the window, and found he couldn't see anything outside except a wall of bright orange.

Rather worried, Fortyodd took the door off its hinges and found that the doorway was completely blocked by the biggest pumpkin he had ever seen. It was acres across from side to side. Fortyodd squeezed out of the doorway and climbed up onto the top of the enormous vegetable.

High up on top, it was like standing on an orange mountain, and there were several other orange mountains next to it. The huge pumpkins completely surrounded his garden shed, and seemed in danger of crushing it.

The formula had certainly worked.

Fortyodd wasn't really sure what to do next, but he knew that, one way or another, it would involve a lot of pumpkin-eating.

Everyone thereabouts agreed that Fortyodd's pumpkins were the biggest Big Veg they had ever seen. People flocked from miles around to see them. Families of giants had their photographs taken posing in front of the great pumpkin range. Passing dragons looked down at the pumpkins in astonishment. Dwarf mountaineers climbed them and stuck flags in the top.

Twoscore's prize cabbages won the Big Veg rosette at the Harvest Show, of course. Everyone said it was a shame. Fortyodd's pumpkins were the biggest in the world, but even with his friend Fiftytimes' help, he couldn't budge them an inch, let alone take them to the show! Still, he knew one thing — his grandfather would have been proud of him!

THE SMALLEST GIANT

WRITTEN BY DAVE KING

Albert the Giant had a big problem. Or rather, he had a little problem that was, in fact, a big problem! And if all that sounds a trifle confusing, imagine how poor Albert felt.

Albert's problem was this: he wasn't a very big giant. Now, if you or I were to look at Albert, we would definitely say he was a big giant. Certainly, if you were to invite him round for tea at your house, you would soon see how big Albert was when he couldn't get in through the front door — in fact, he'd probably be taller than your entire house.

But in the Land of the Giants (a place not too far from the Land of the Pixies and just to the right of Fairyland — you can't miss it because it's well signposted from the motorway) there were some really, really, really tall giants. These were not the kind of giants you would choose to pick a fight with, as you might end up with a sore nose (unless, of course, you happen to be an even taller giant).

So, although Albert was undeniably a giant, in comparison to most of his friends he was a very short giant indeed!

As you can imagine, this led to one or two problems for Albert. Some of the other, taller giants would tease Albert. "Ha!" they would say. "Call yourself a giant — a giant elf maybe! Perhaps you should go and live in the Land of the Pixies, with all the other little people!"

Albert would hang his head in shame. This kind of talk made him feel very sad, and sometimes a big fat tear would roll down his cheek. He wished he could be the same size as all the others and he had tried all sorts of things to make himself grow. He had even visited a wise old witch in Fairyland, but the spell she gave him just made his nose grow longer and longer, so he'd had to go back and get the spell reversed. But generally speaking, he was a happy giant, and he did his best to keep cheerful about things.

One day, Albert was sitting at home reading a copy of *Gnomes and Gardens* magazine — a publication that delved into the lives and homes of gnomes, elves, pixies, fairies, sprites and all manner of little, magical people. It was a favourite of Albert's, as reading about people smaller than himself usually made him feel really rather tall. Suddenly, he heard a dreadful commotion coming from outside his house. He rushed over to the window only to discover that his view was blocked by masses of other giants, out in the street.

He tore open the front door and tried to push his way through the crowd. "Excuse me!" he shouted. "What's going on? What are you all looking at?"

But it was no use. The crowd of giants, with their backs to Albert, were cheering too loudly. If you've ever heard one giant shout, you're probably deaf by now! Just imagine how loud a whole crowd of giants can be … loud enough to knock your next door neighbour's wig off, I'll guarantee!

Whatever was happening in the middle of the street, it was making the giants very excited. Albert didn't want to miss all the fun, so he dropped down onto his hands and knees and began to weave his way between the legs of the crowd. After a while he reached the front of the crowd, and through the tangle of legs he could see a big crowd on the other side of the street, equally excited and equally noisy.

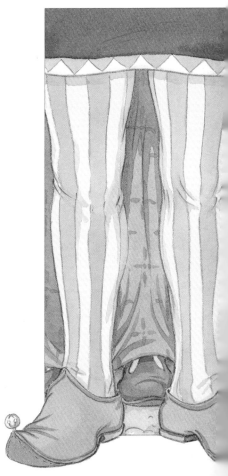

Albert tilted his head to one side and listened. Just above the roar of the crowd he could hear something. It sounded like … it was … yes, Albert could definitely hear the sound of a trumpet! He wiggled through the rest of the crowd and stood up. The sight that greeted him as he looked down the street was a grand one. Smiling regally from inside his royal carriage, the King of the Giants was leading a grand parade through the streets of the town. It was the tenth anniversary of the King's coronation, and he was leading the way to an enormous party being held in his honour. The King was a real sight to see, bedecked in jewels from top to toe and with a gleaming crown. "I bet that cost him a few week's pocket money!" Albert thought, as he stared at the King's finery.

Now it just so happened that for the past few weeks, King Bill the Second had been on a diet. He was rather fond of food, to say the least.

It was nothing for him to eat two chickens, a raspberry trifle, a plate of chips, three doughnuts and a chocolate fudge cake all in one go. And that was just for breakfast!

"You must get some exercise, and lose some weight!" Doctor Harold, the Royal Physician had told him. "And if I might suggest…" the doctor continued, holding up a videotape, "I've just brought out my own exercise tape, *Lose Weight the Harold Way*! Only nine pounds, ninety nine pence to you, Sire!"

Even after the doctor had been thrown out into the street, the medical man's words rang true in the King's ears as he looked down at his flabby waist. He decided to go on a diet, cutting down on all the cakes and sweets that he liked to munch on during his favourite television shows, eating more sensibly and even taking a little, just a little, mind … exercise.

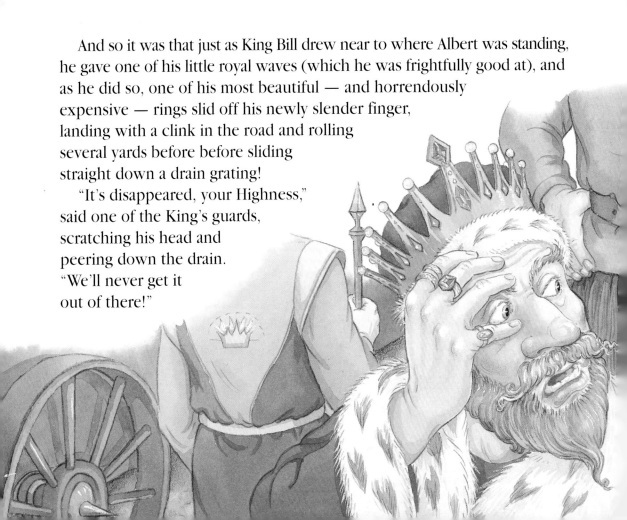

And so it was that just as King Bill drew near to where Albert was standing, he gave one of his little royal waves (which he was frightfully good at), and as he did so, one of his most beautiful — and horrendously expensive — rings slid off his newly slender finger, landing with a clink in the road and rolling several yards before before sliding straight down a drain grating!

"It's disappeared, your Highness," said one of the King's guards, scratching his head and peering down the drain. "We'll never get it out of there!"

The King let out a terrible shriek. "My ring!" he cried. "Oh woe! Truly my ring is lost for ever!" Albert thought the King was over-reacting a bit. He watched as the other giants took turns to try and pull the grate up from the drain. They huffed and they puffed, but try as they might, it just wouldn't budge. "There will be no more festivities until my ring is found," declared the King.

Albert decided it was time to help out. "Um… excuse me, I'm sorry to bother you, your Majesty, but I think I might be able to help!" Albert said politely (he was a particularly polite giant, you see).

King Bill looked down his long, regal nose at Albert. "You?" he said, snootily. "But you're only a little giant! How can you possibly help?"

Without answering, Albert squeezed his small arm through the grate and, after a bit of puffing and grunting (although it might have been a bit of grunting and puffing, you can never be sure in cases like these), he pulled out the King's ring!

The King snatched his ring, and without a word of thanks, waved his carriage on down the street with more than a dash of pomp. This was a very rude thing for the King to do, certainly, but king's are like that sometimes. More importantly, however, all the other giants saw what Albert had done, and lifting him high on their shoulders, cheered louder than ever because Albert had saved the day. The party lasted all night, and from that day forward no one ever teased Albert about being small again!